TINYWORDS

ISSUE 10.3

AUTUMN, 2010

TINYWORDS 10.3: AUTUMN, 2010

This issue was originally published on tinywords.com from October 10 to December 30, 2010, and is archived at http://tinywords.com/category/issue-10-3/.

Editor and publisher: d. f. tweney

Assistant editors: Peter Newton, David Serjeant, John Emil Vincent

ISSN 2157-5010

ISBN 978-1-257-85729-6

EDITOR'S NOTE

This issue has an urban theme, so most of the selections have to do with cities (even if very loosely).

I'm very proud of the poetry in this issue. Once again we were overwhelmed by the quantity and quality of submissions, and it was difficult to say no to many of them. I think that the 50-odd poems we've selected are very good, and I hope you'll agree.

This issue would not have been possible without the enthusiastic, able, and intelligent help of assistant editors Peter Newton, David Serjeant and John Emil Vincent.

I'm grateful to the editors for their help, and to all who submitted poems for consideration.

—D. F. TWENEY

  s

                                              d

                                        r

                                        i

                                        b

recession rising from the factory stacks five small black

                                        —*ED MARKOWSKI*

4

October chill
the silence in this shadow

—*MARTIN GOTTLIEB COHEN*

homeless ...
a plastic bag drifts
across the sidewalk

—*DIETMAR TAUCHNER*

sunrise
from village to village
a rooster's crow

—*Bouwe Brouwer*

heat wave
at the big city
flower market
ten thousand shades
of radiant yellow

—*Margarita Engle*

migrating geese
rising
out of my chair

—JIM KACIAN

slowly
two clouds collide
over rush hour

—*C. P. HARRISON*

dense fog
the train evaporates
into a distant horn

—*Kala Ramesh*

flea market~
every old watch
keeps its time

—*Dana-Maria Onica*

moonrise
moonset
your nakedness

—*Charles Trumbull*

autumn afternoon—
an empty shopping cart
waits at the bus stop

—*ALEXA SELPH*

dusk—
ten thousand blackbirds
and no place to park

—*C. P. HARRISON*

lit fish stall
open mouths darken
in the night

—*MARTIN GOTTLIEB COHEN*

GOGYOHKA

she slips
into the blue haze
of memory
Staten Island
Ferry

—*CAROLE JOHNSTON*

clear   settles

night   on

my   a

moon   white

shadow   tombstone

—*ED MARKOWSKI*

deep breath
before I enter
the panhandler's aura

—*CHRISTOPHER PICKSLAY*

election night smoke from an unseen cigar

—*JIM KACIAN*

in the distance gunshots opening the dark

—*Marjorie Buettner*

a gardener
on the radio
smells the jasmine

—Marisa Fazio

where street meets sunrise—
the steam

—*C. P. HARRISON*

traffic jam—
my thoughts
still in motion

—*Andrea Cecon*

a yellow leaf
describes the course
of the wind

—*HELEN RUGGIERI*

amid fallen leaves

a business card

still doing its job

—*Janice Campbell*

prayer candle
shadows pass through
each other

—*MARTIN GOTTLIEB COHEN*

HAIKU

I'm not a poem.
I'm a dog. Respect
The differences.

—*RICK MOODY*

Pelham Parkway
between the winter trees
the child's breath

—*MARTIN GOTTLIEB COHEN*

morning walk
at the crossroads
my thoughts
flow
in Spanglish

—*MARGARITA ENGLE*

in the pool
of the ruined resort
the wild ducks

—*JIM KACIAN*

commuter platform
a harmonica blowing
the freight train blues

—*LORIN FORD*

leaving the Tokyo subway,
a hundred umbrellas
rise in unison

—*SIDNEY BENDING*

AT HOME

bay window
no matter the season
drawn curtains

he's not what you'd call sociable. sometimes he just starts
yelling for no reason. but there's no way to predict when
that will be. so how do i explain him to someone new?
someone not in the family? quirky doesn't really cut it.

filling the length
of the front window
blue hydrangea

—ROBERTA BEARY

rooftop garden—
climbing the stairs
back to nature

—*CLAUDETTE RUSSELL*

gallery tour
the ladies gaze
at the dozing watchman

—*Barry Goodmann*

park bench
pigeons begging
the homeless man

—*JEFF HOAGLAND*

department store sale flyers flying

—*SIDNEY BENDING*

hotel bar:

                      ice shifts

and shifts again.

—*JOHN PAPPAS*

just a flat tire
chained to a lamppost
waning autumn moon

—*BARRY GOODMANN*

dead birds at the base
of the lit skyscraper
autumn midnight

—*George Swede*

footprints
the prairie dog stretches
its shadow

—*MARTIN GOTTLIEB COHEN*

deep snow ...
the acorn
up to its cap

—*STANFORD M. FORRESTER*

funeral procession the hitchhiker tucks his thumbs in
his pockets

—*ED MARKOWSKI*

nor'easter—
scent of the river
rising

—*KATHE L. PALKA*

sheltered by the bus stop empties

—*Jim Kacian*

Buddha eyes—
a hunchbacked woman sweeps
the temple steps

—*BRUCE H. FEINGOLD*

lovers' moon—
a cicada leaves its shell
on the fence post

—*Kathe L. Palka*

birthday party
the new neighbor
shows his tattoo

—*MARLEEN HULST*

SIGHT UNSEEN

my maternal grandfather passed away on june 22 1980
from black lung thanks to 16 years of drilling chopping &
chipping coal down in the guts of the white star mineral
company's mine number 21 & 40 years of sniffing soot
smoking steel & swallowing fire in the foundry at the
crown jewel of old mister henry ford's empire ..... the
rouge plant .....

i was 25 .... i was back in town from reno ... i was what the
cat dragged in .... i was slashed the slash & the blade i
was the the fist ... the gloves .... i was the punch ....

i had blasted off from planet catholic when the calendar
claimed i was 16 .... bob dylan bonnie bramlett john
lennon & grace slick were ...... the lord the nun the pope
the virgin mother & ...... more than enough religion to last
a lifetime

the day before the funeral my mother called ....

"the funeral is yesterday" "the funeral is today" "the
funeral is tomorrow" "eddie we're all going to
communion" "it would be respectful if you went" "grandpa
will be so proud" she went on ......

"all night tonight you should beg god for mercy" "make
sure you dress nice" "make sure you shave" "no jeans no
tennis shoes no t-shirt wear socks" "no buddha swinging
smiling & swaying on that chain"

and on ......

"no liquor on your breath no humming purple haze" "no
talking politics no ronnie reagan jokes"
and on ....

"leave your good time charlie slut marcia home" "cousin
lena wants to fix you up" "cousin lena wants to fix you up
with cousin gina"

and on ....

"my god eddie at least make it seem like you're ...."

i honored each & every one of my mother's requests

and then ...

the wake began.

confessional
  something's still stuck to
    the soles of my wingtips

—ED MARKOWSKI

dead-end street
every house but one
boarded up

—*BRENDAN SLATER*

the writer
we exchange
a few words

—BOUWE BROUWER

trailing the snail
on the pale gray pavement
an ellipsis ...

—*Pat Tompkins*

a bowed head
in each bus window
mountain fog

—*WENDE S. DUFLON*

shortest day—
the waiting room clock
at the ICU

—*Charles Trumbull*

January thaw
dog-walkers greet
leashed strangers

—*ANN K. SCHWADER*

goodbye hugs—
all the places
where we touch

—*Jim Kacian*

not getting my joke
but he smiles anyway—
the stone buddha

—*STANFORD M. FORRESTER*

juncos black
silhouettes in birch trees
notes on a tangled clef

—DAVID CRISTY

cherry

blossoms

drifting

down

mission

street

three

pink

hookers

—*ED MARKOWSKI*

black fedora
the blind man
inspects its brim

—*JOHN STONE*

corner beggar change is everywhere

—*GEORGE SWEDE*

NOTES ON THE POEMS

p. 9 ("migrating geese"): Originally published in *Dim Sum* #2.

p. 11 ("dense fog"): Previously published in *The Heron's Nest*, June 2009.

p. 17: A gogyohka is a form of five-line poetry that originated in Japan in the 1950s.

p. 26 ("amid fallen leaves"): A version of this haiku was previously published in the Texas 09 Haikucalendar.

p. 31 ("in the pool"): Previous publications: Ludbreg Calendar 2001 First Prize; *Iz Kamna; long after.*

p. 45 ("nor'easter"): Previously published in *The River*.

p. 46 ("sheltered"): Originally published in *where i leave off / waar ik ophoud.*

p. 58 ("goodbye hugs"): Previously published in *ant4; antbook; border lands.*

p. 62 ("black fedora"): First published in *tinywords* in 2007, and later appeared *in Simply Haiku*, 2008.

www.ingramcontent.com/pod-product-compliance
Lightning Source LLC
Chambersburg PA
CBHW060427050426
42449CB00009B/2177